The pictures in this book are the illustrations in the book below.

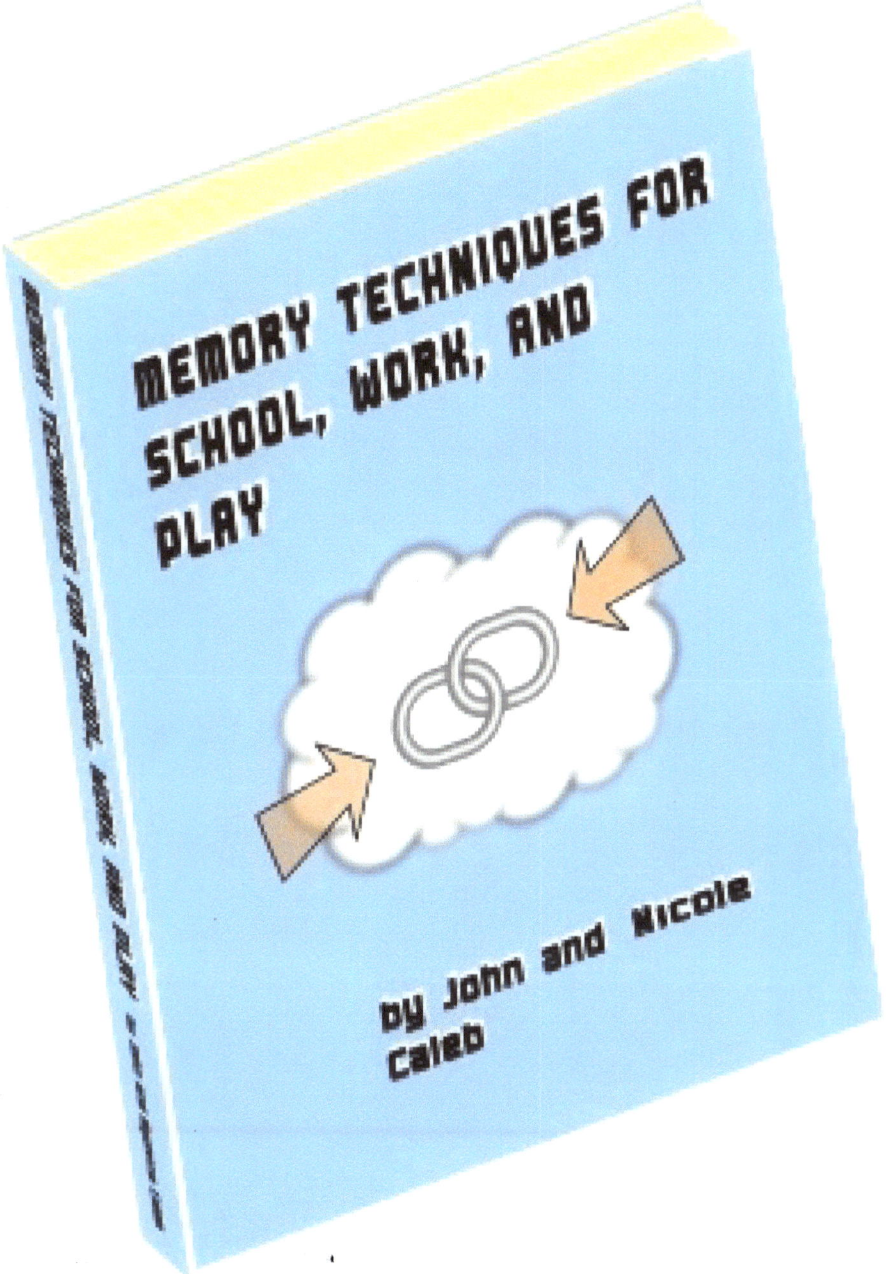

MEMORY TECHNIQUES FOR SCHOOL, WORK, AND PLAY

by John and Nicole Caleb

TABLE OF CONTENTS

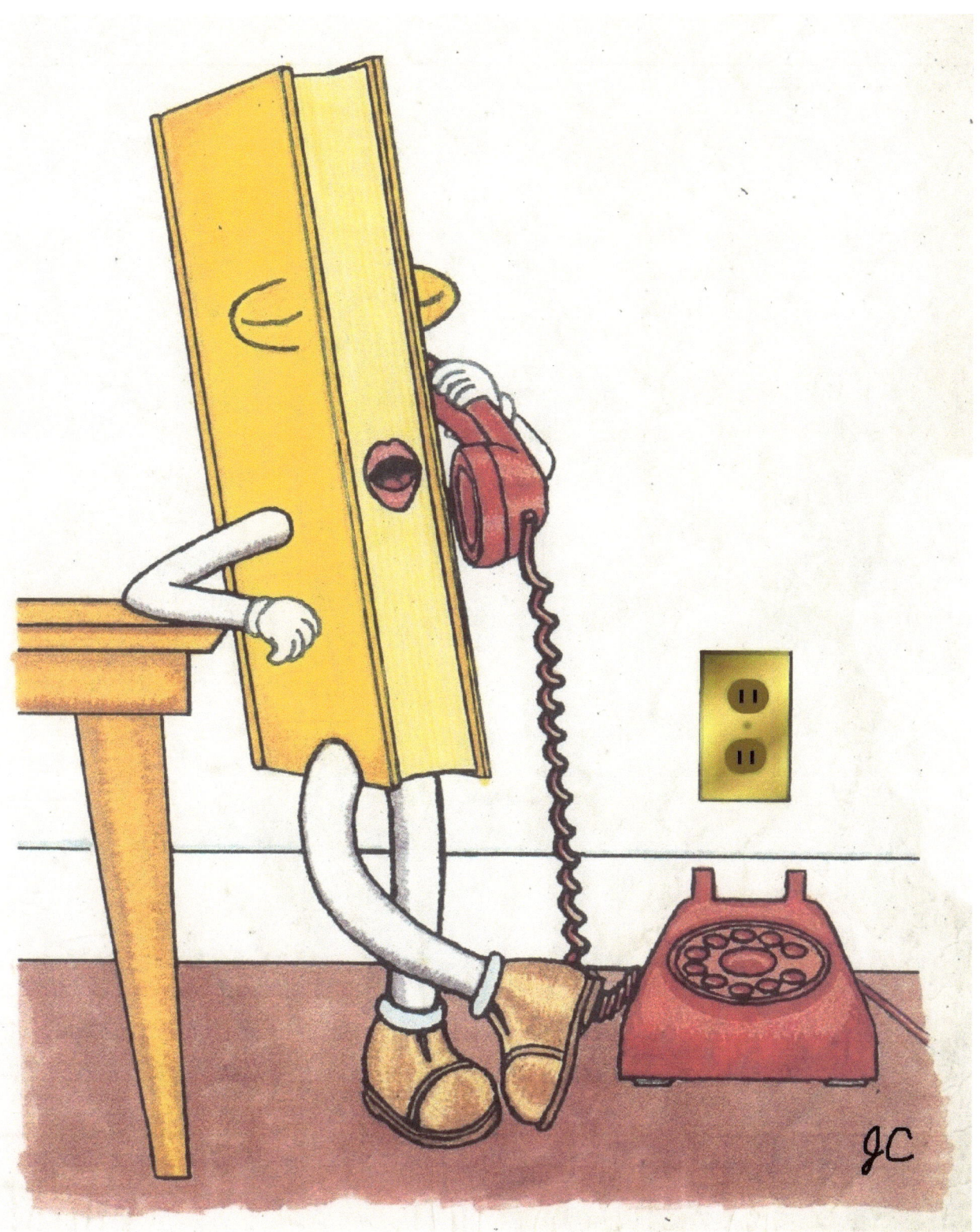

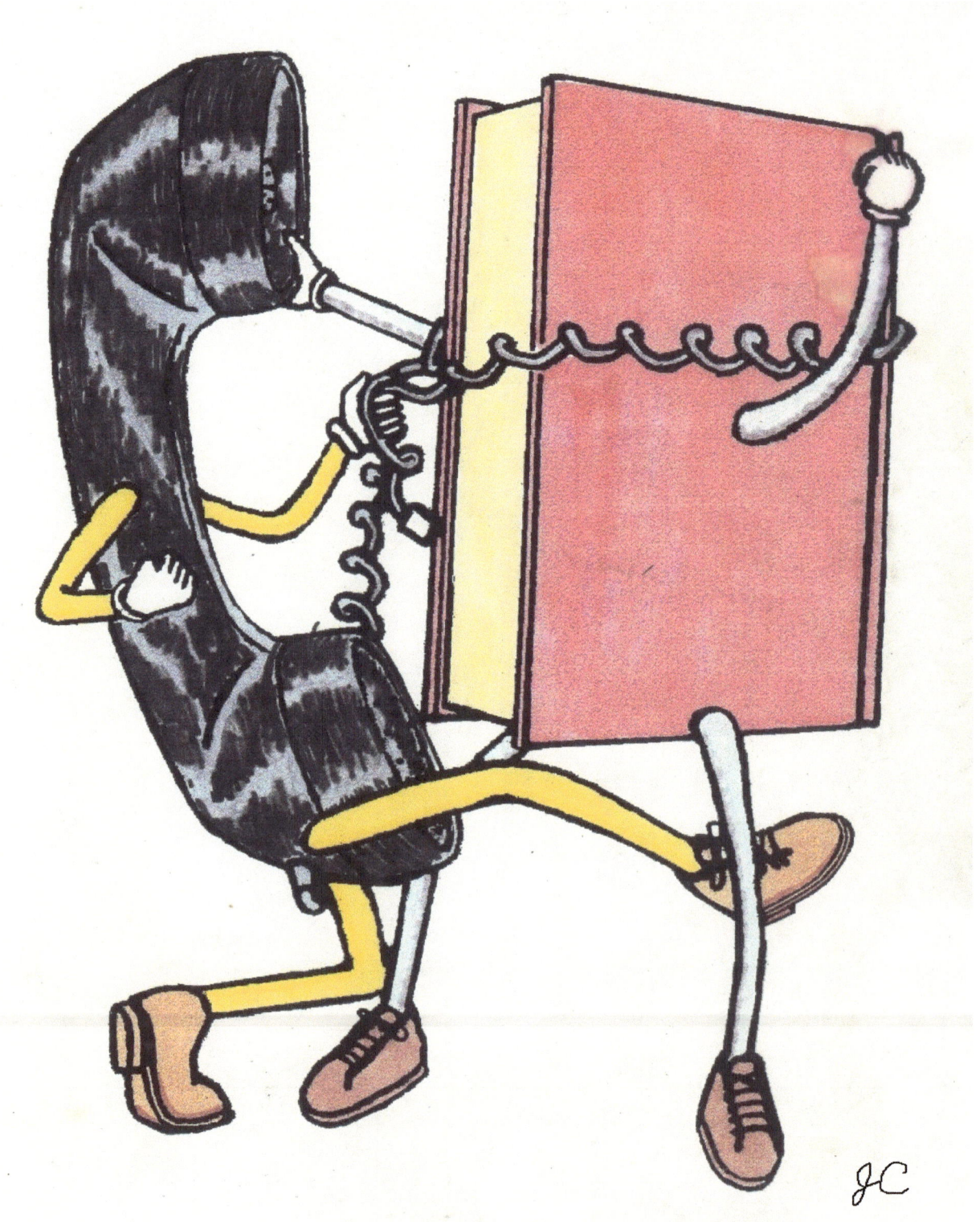

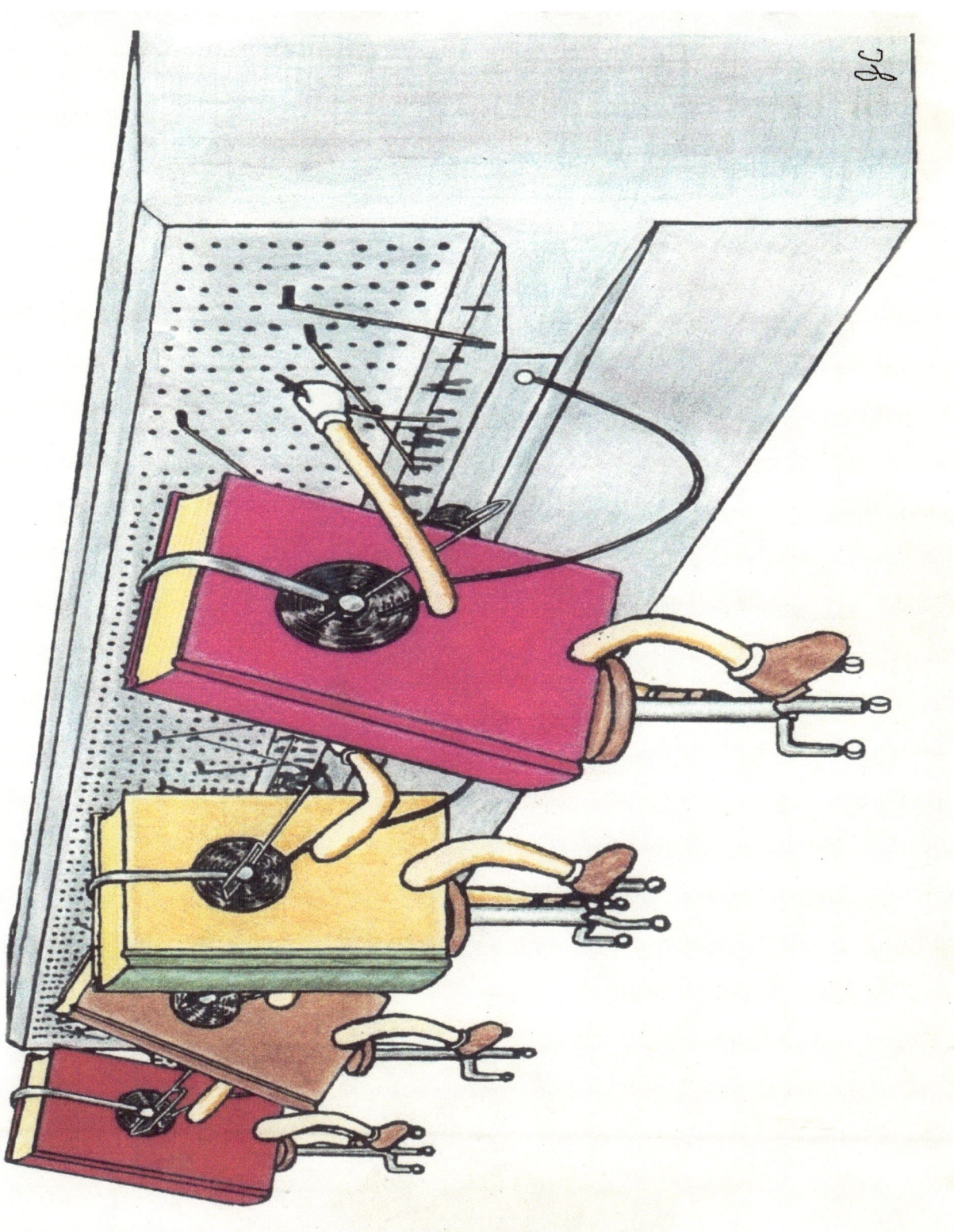

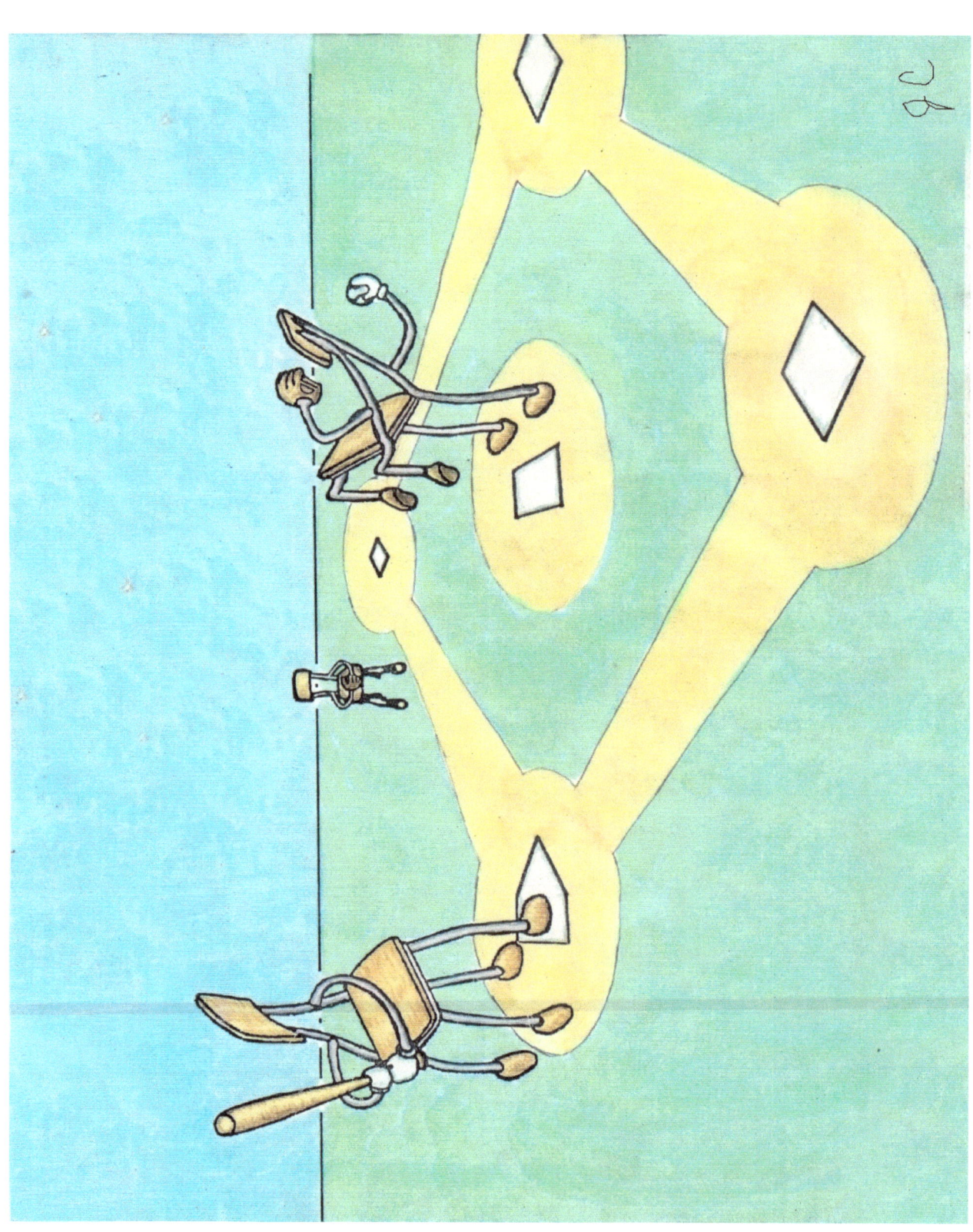

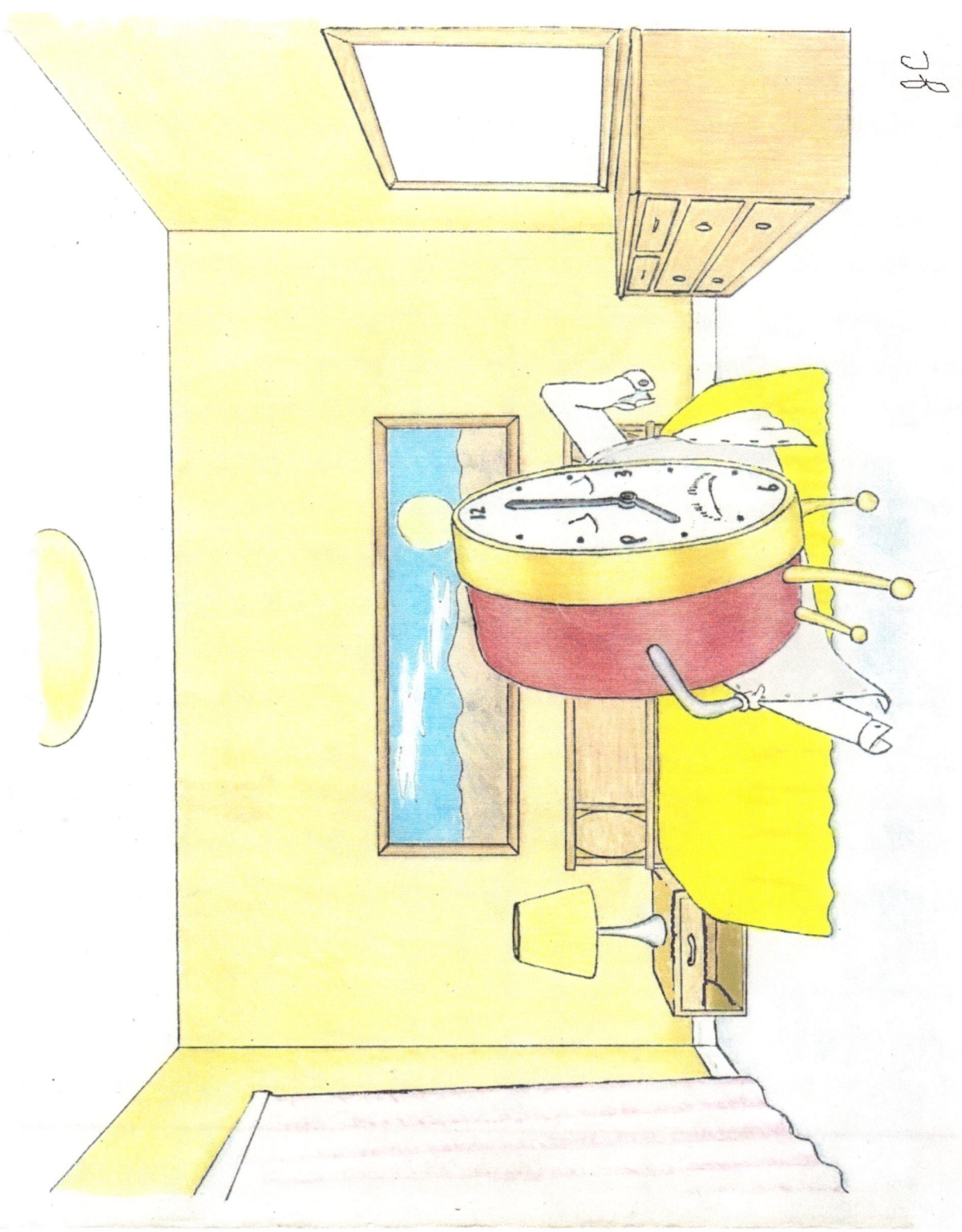

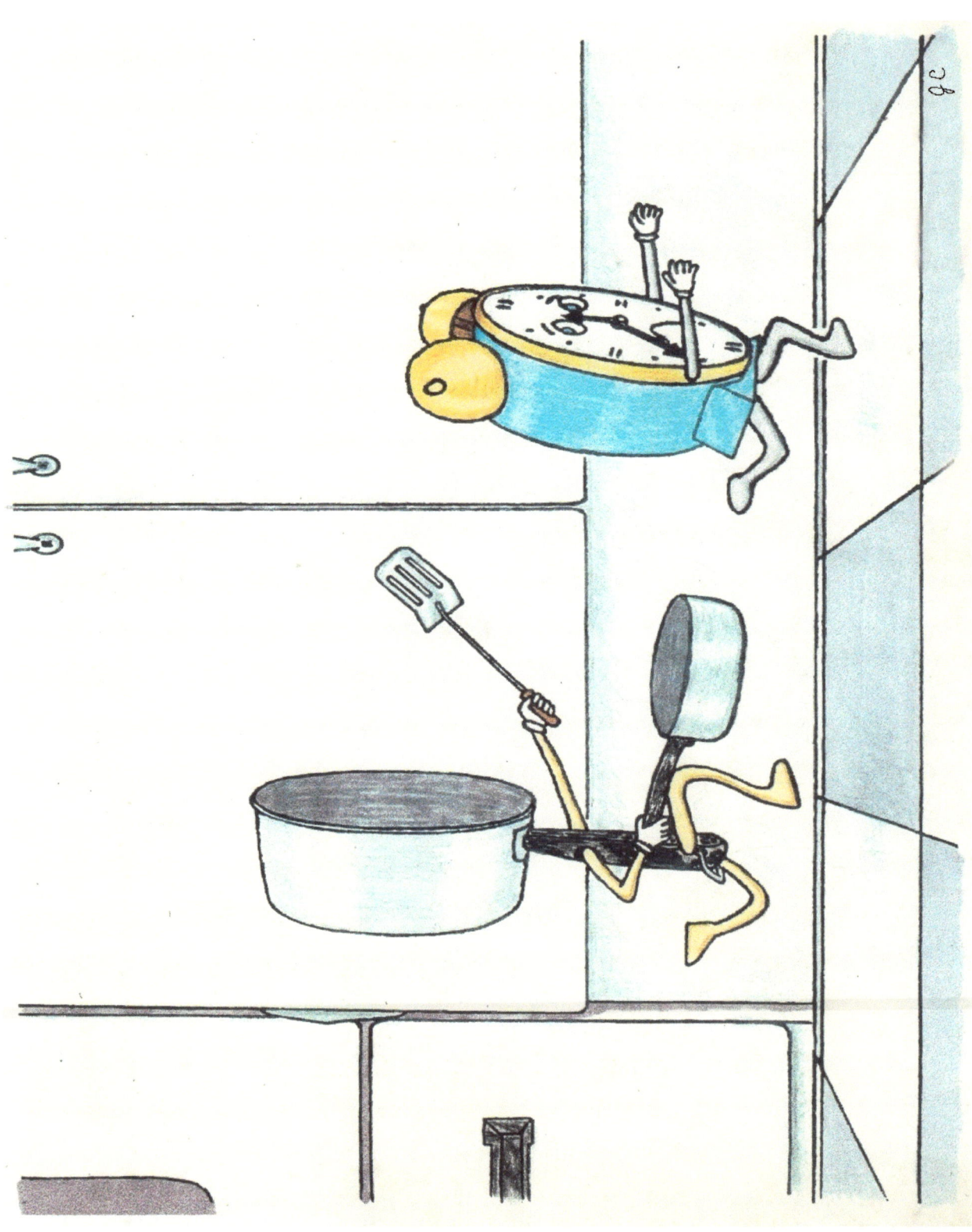

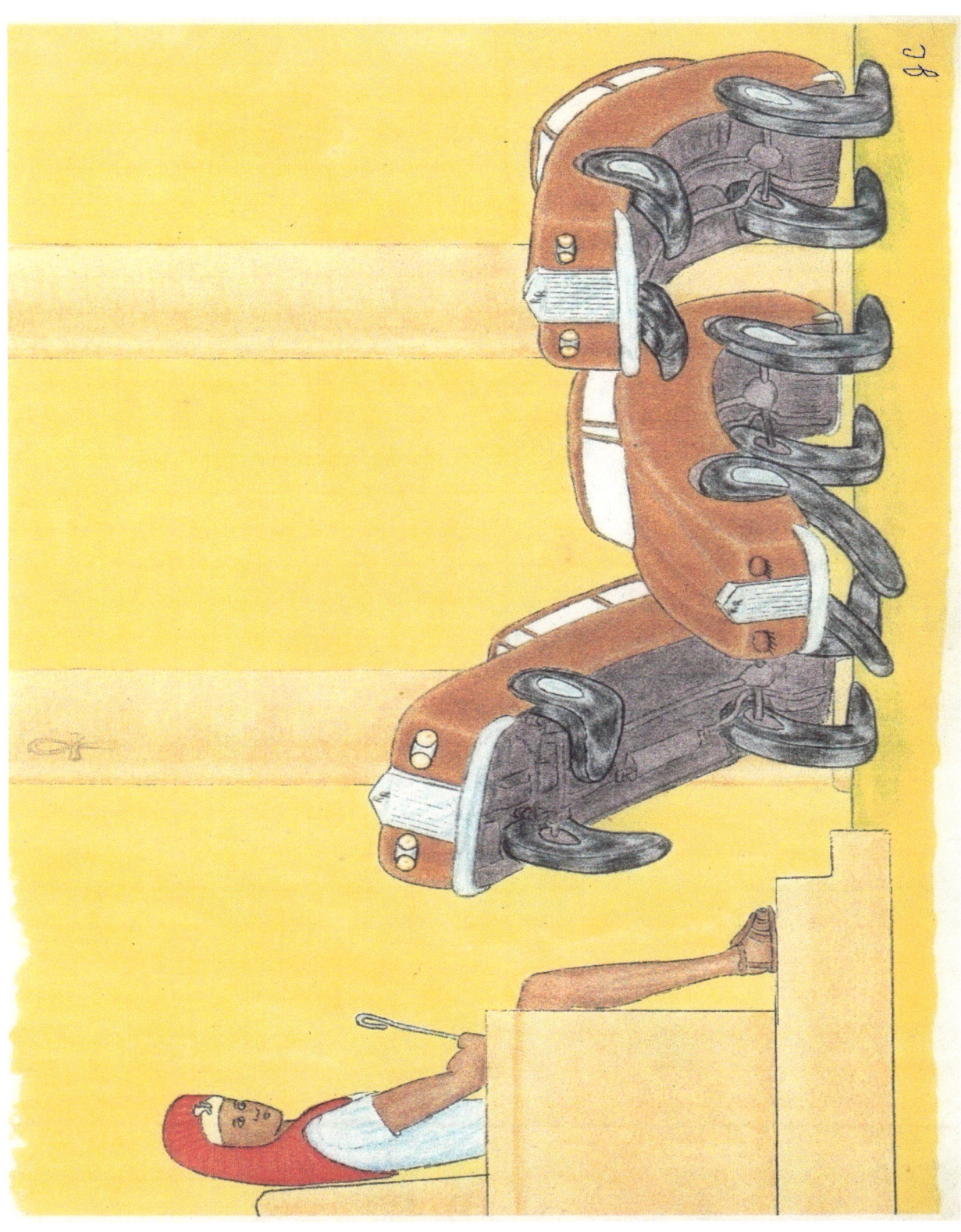

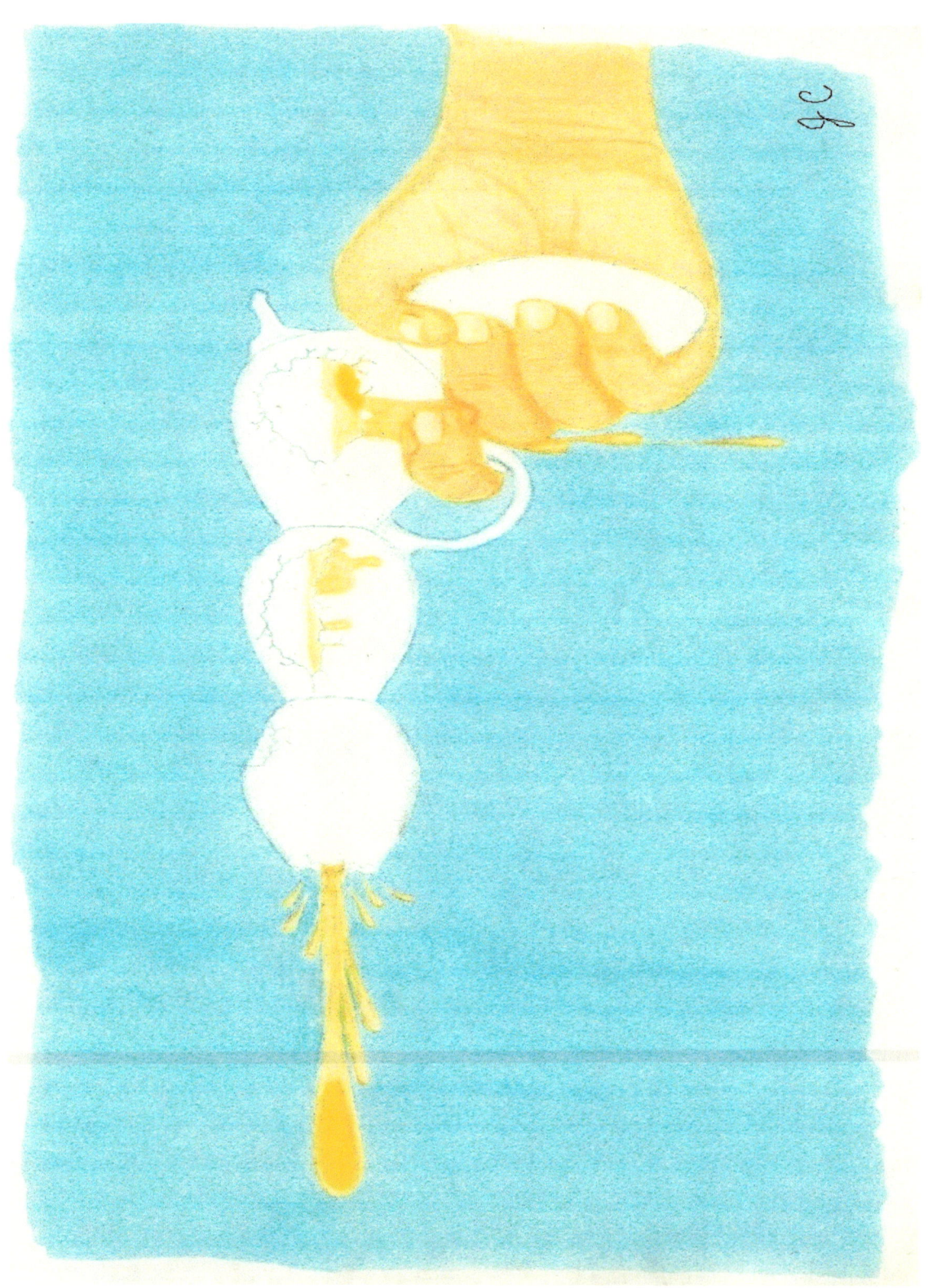

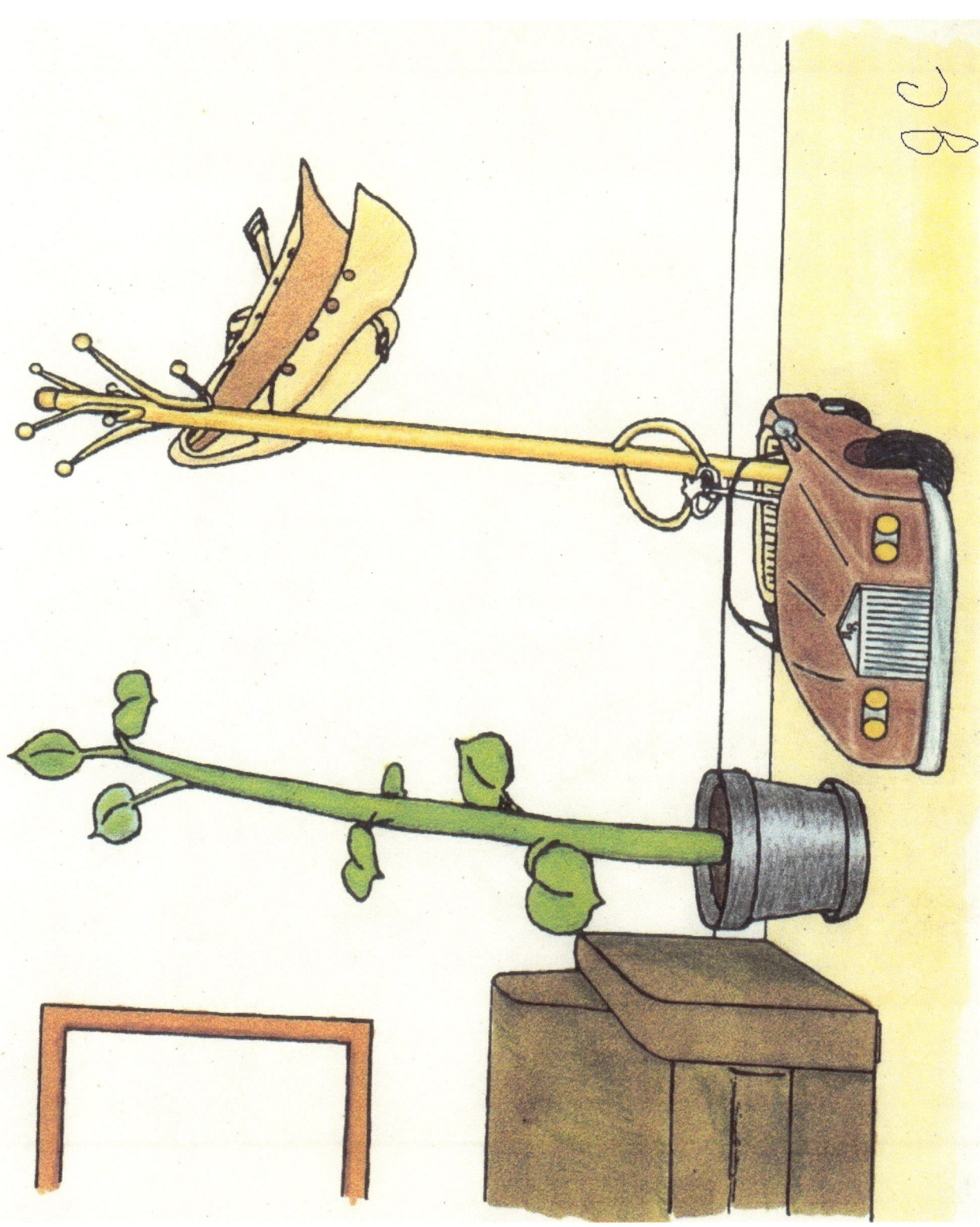

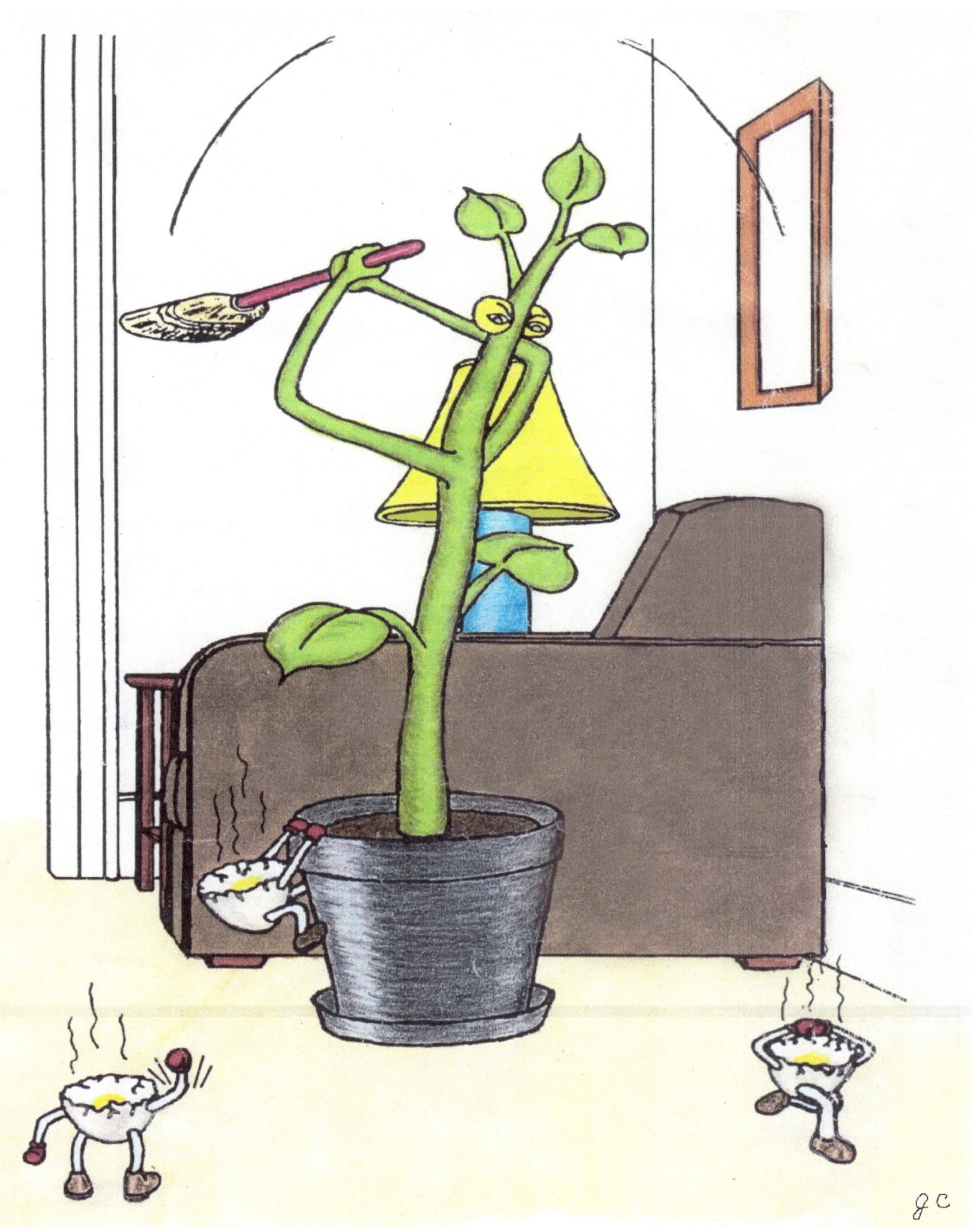

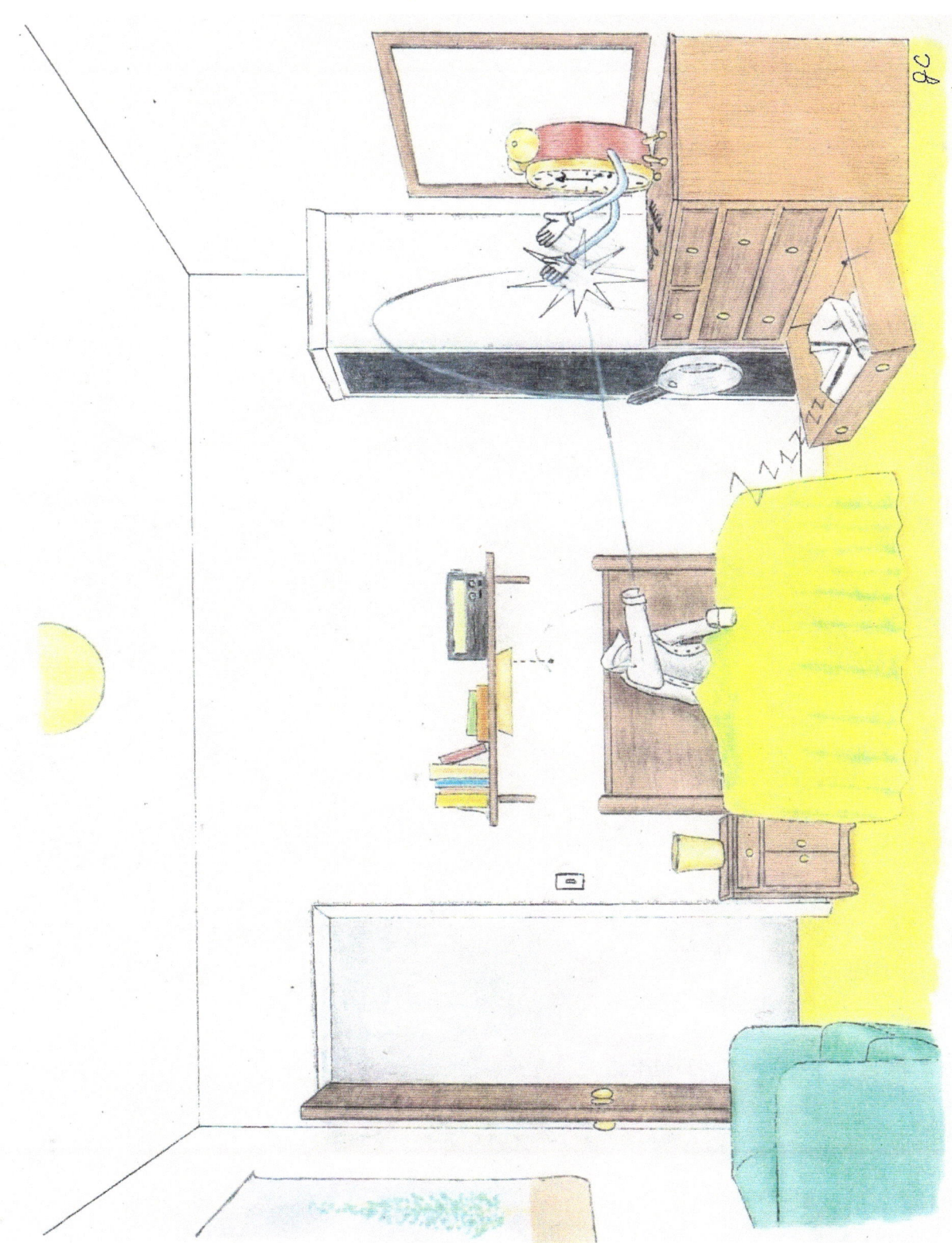

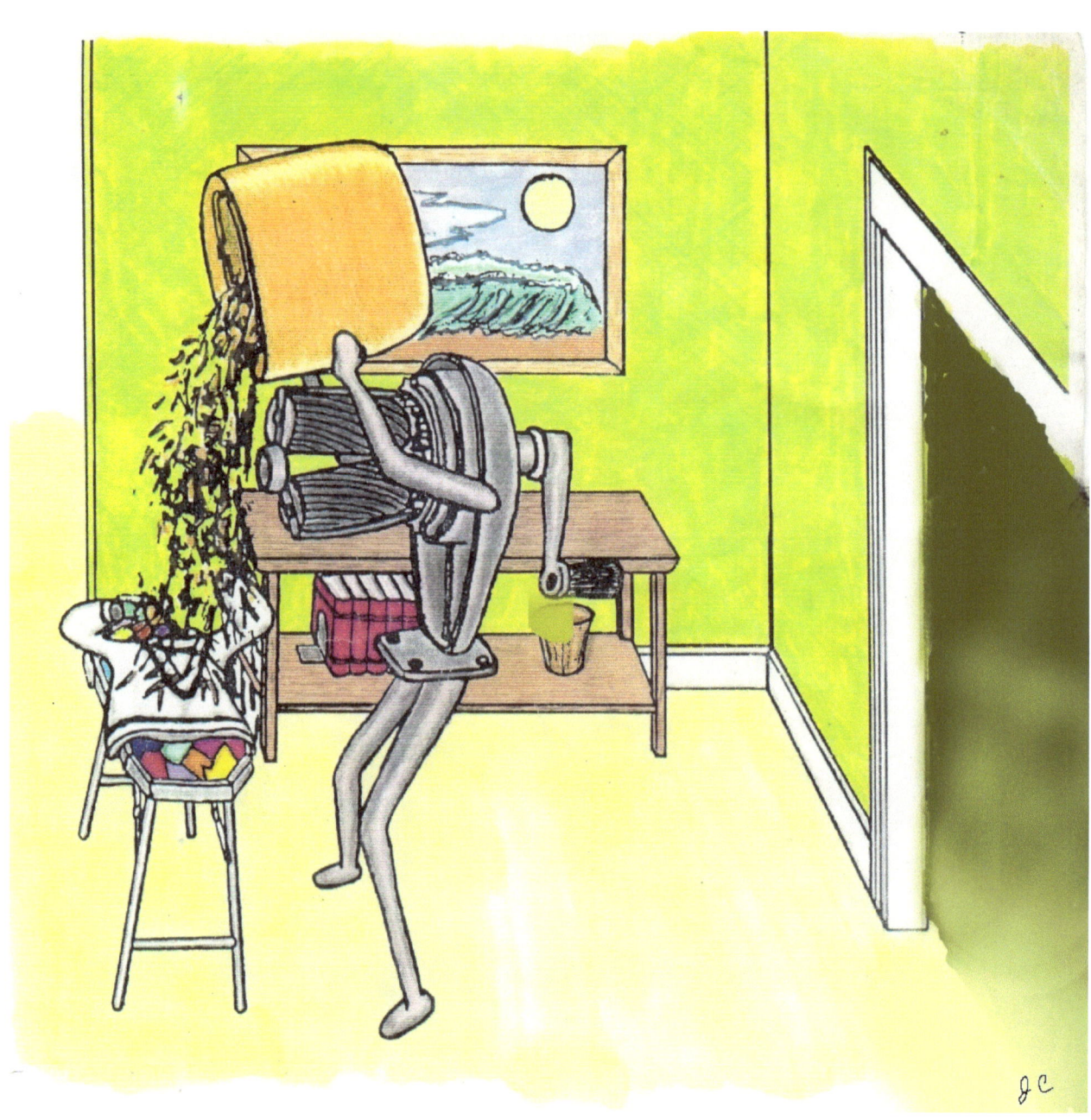

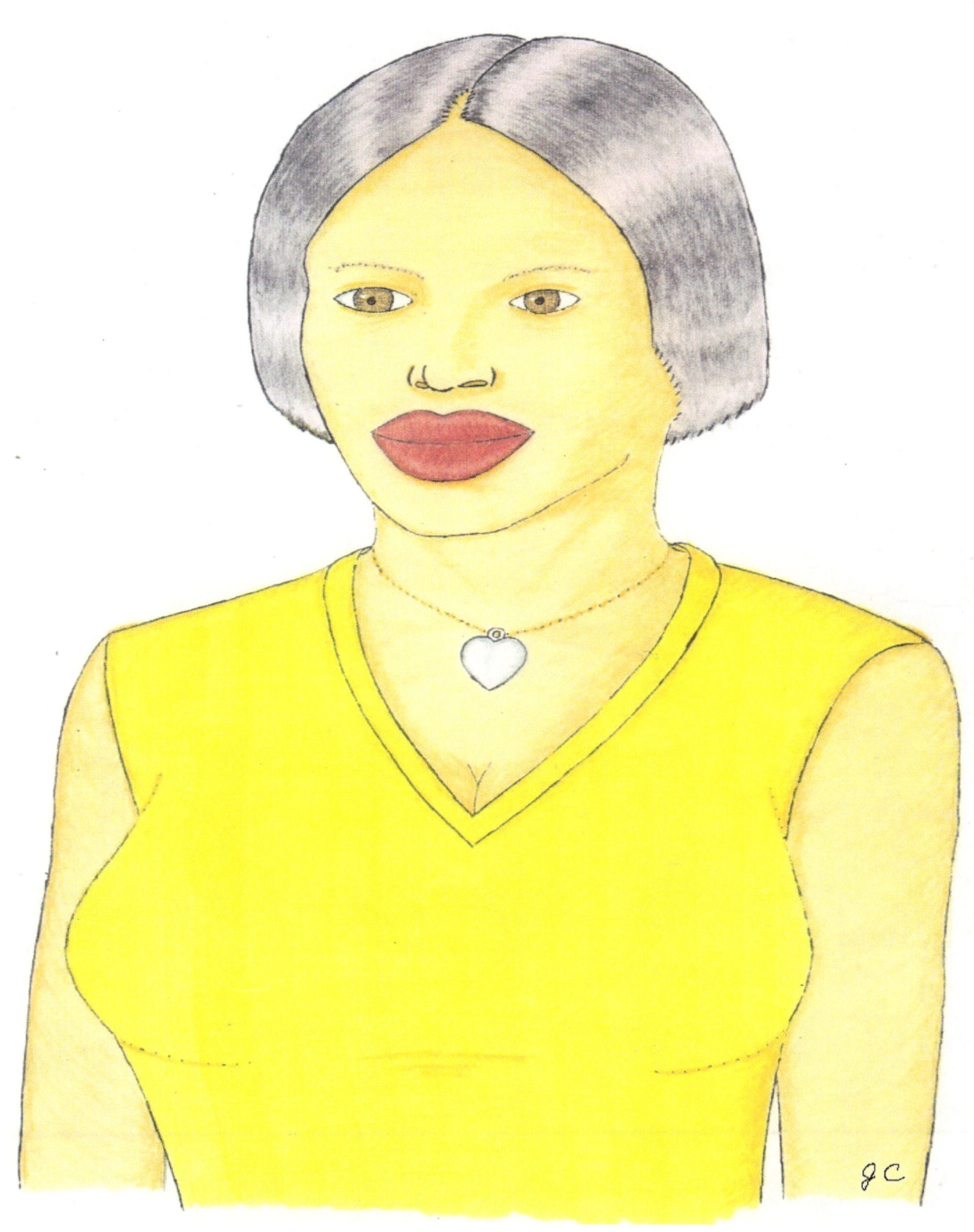

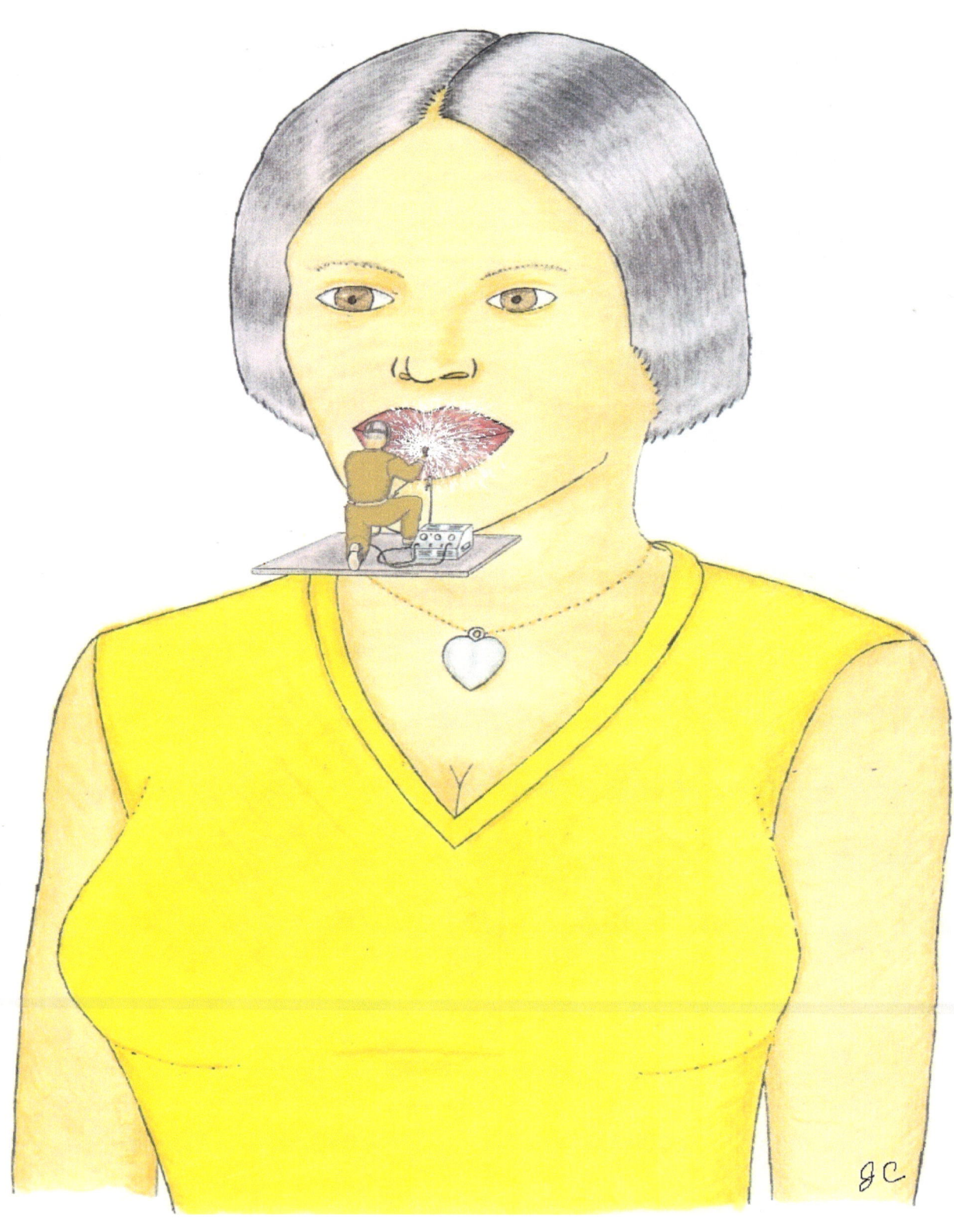

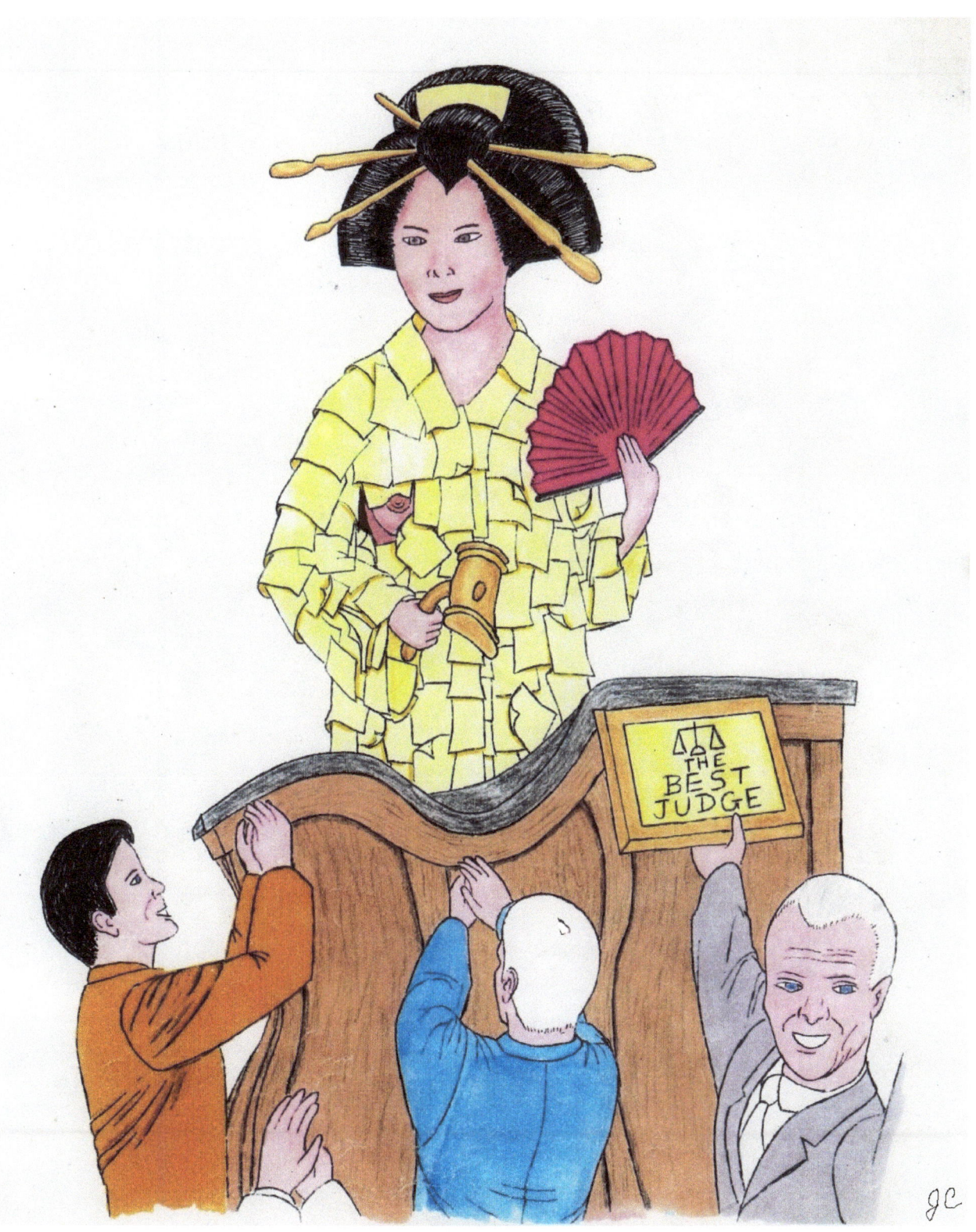

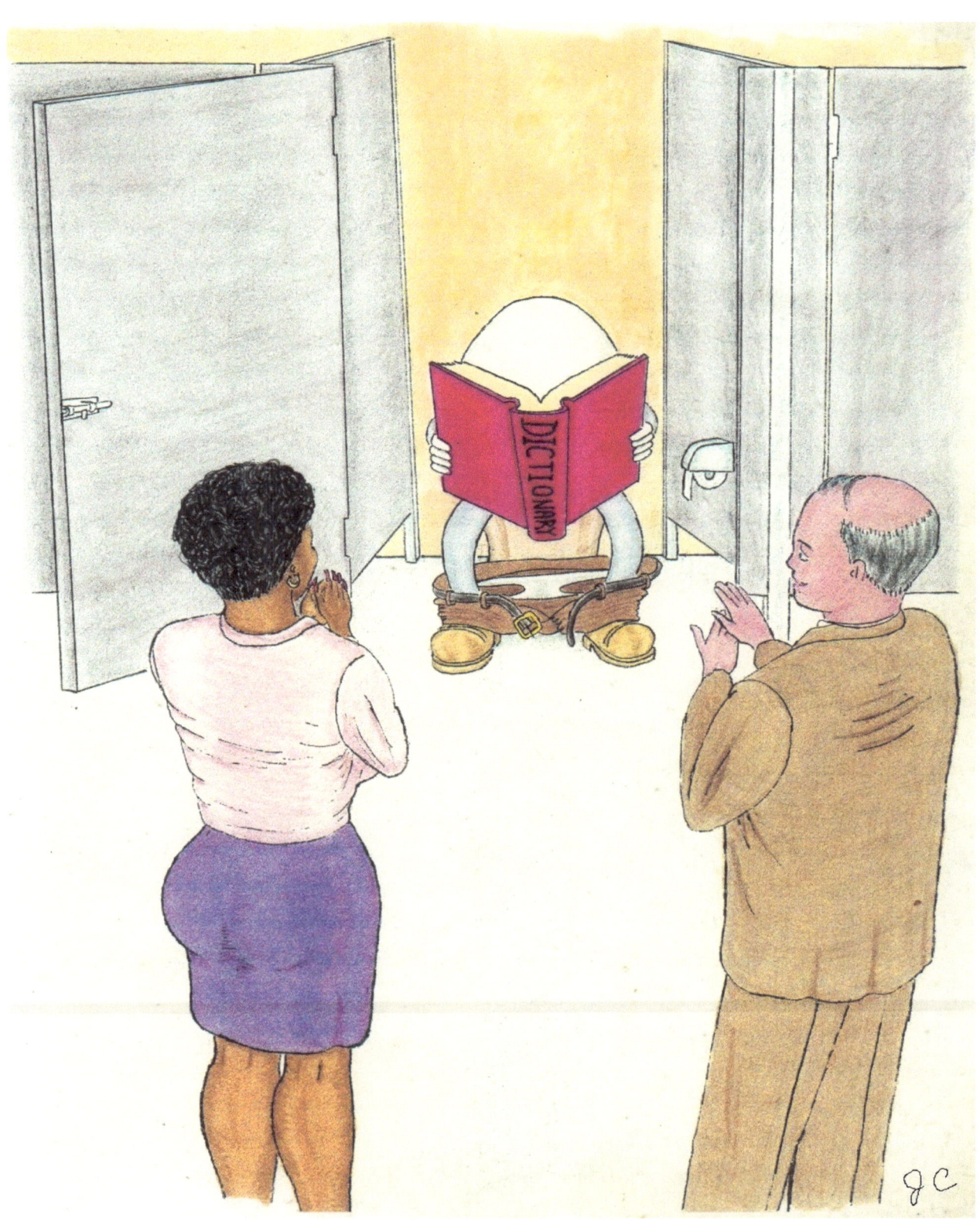

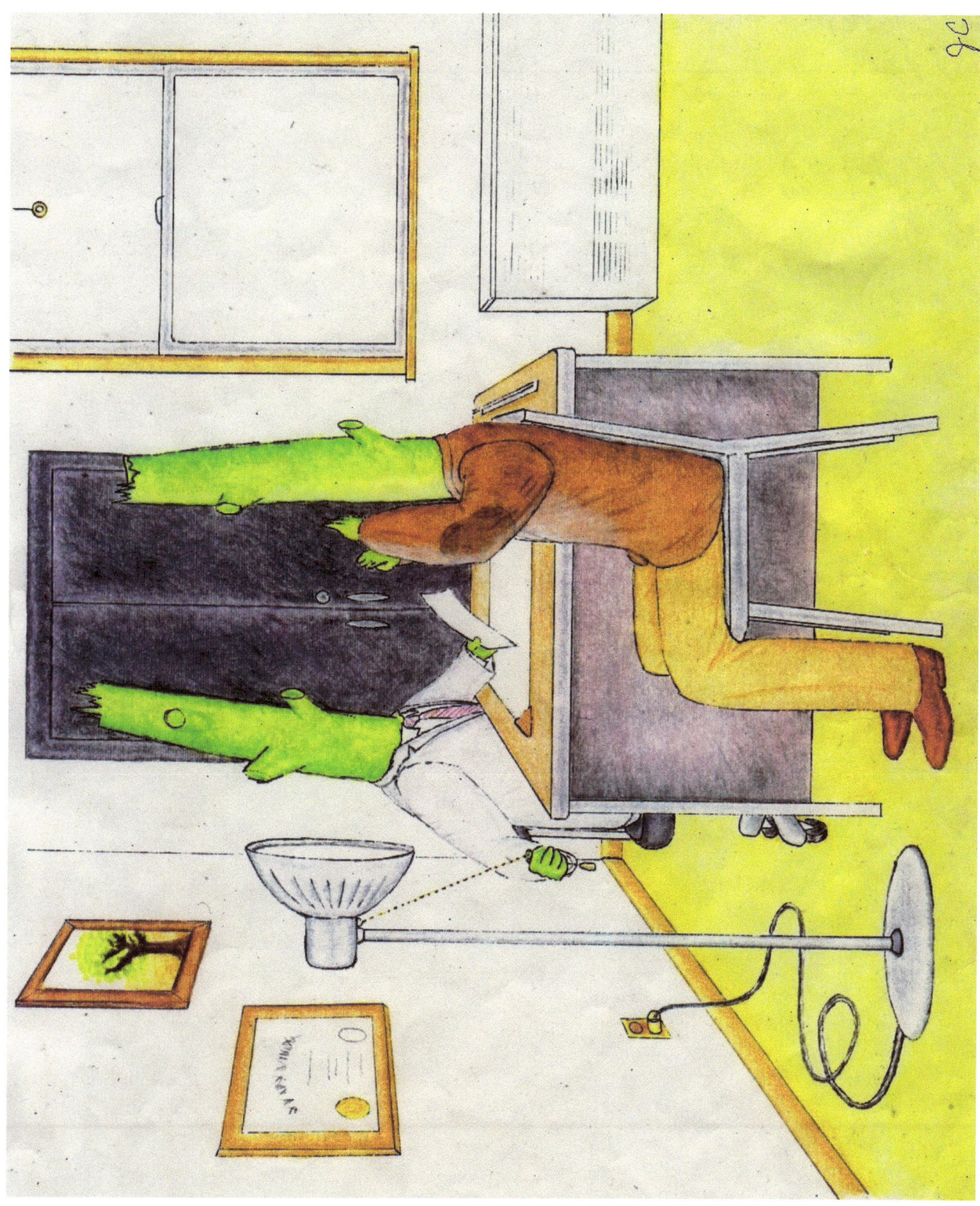

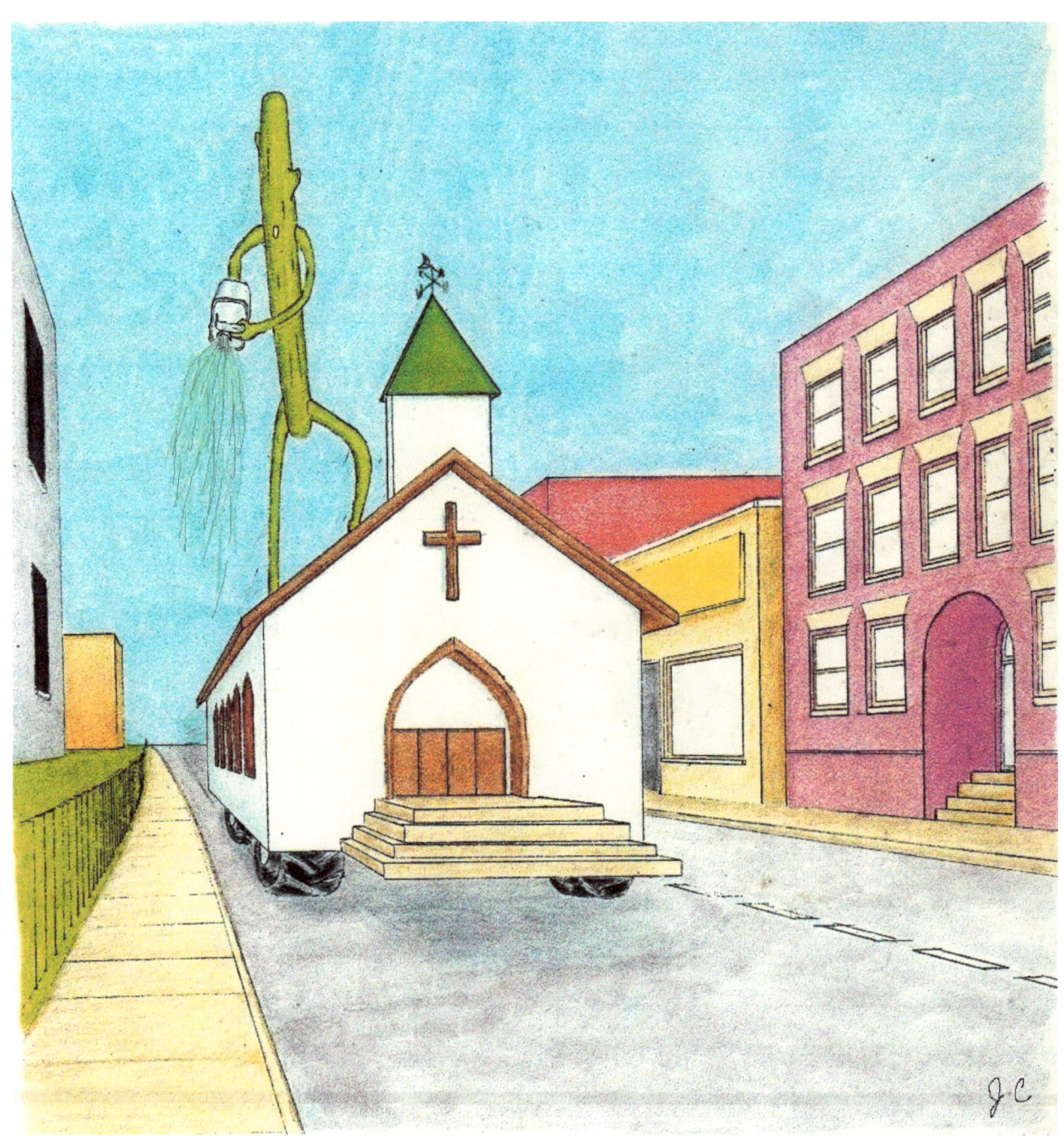

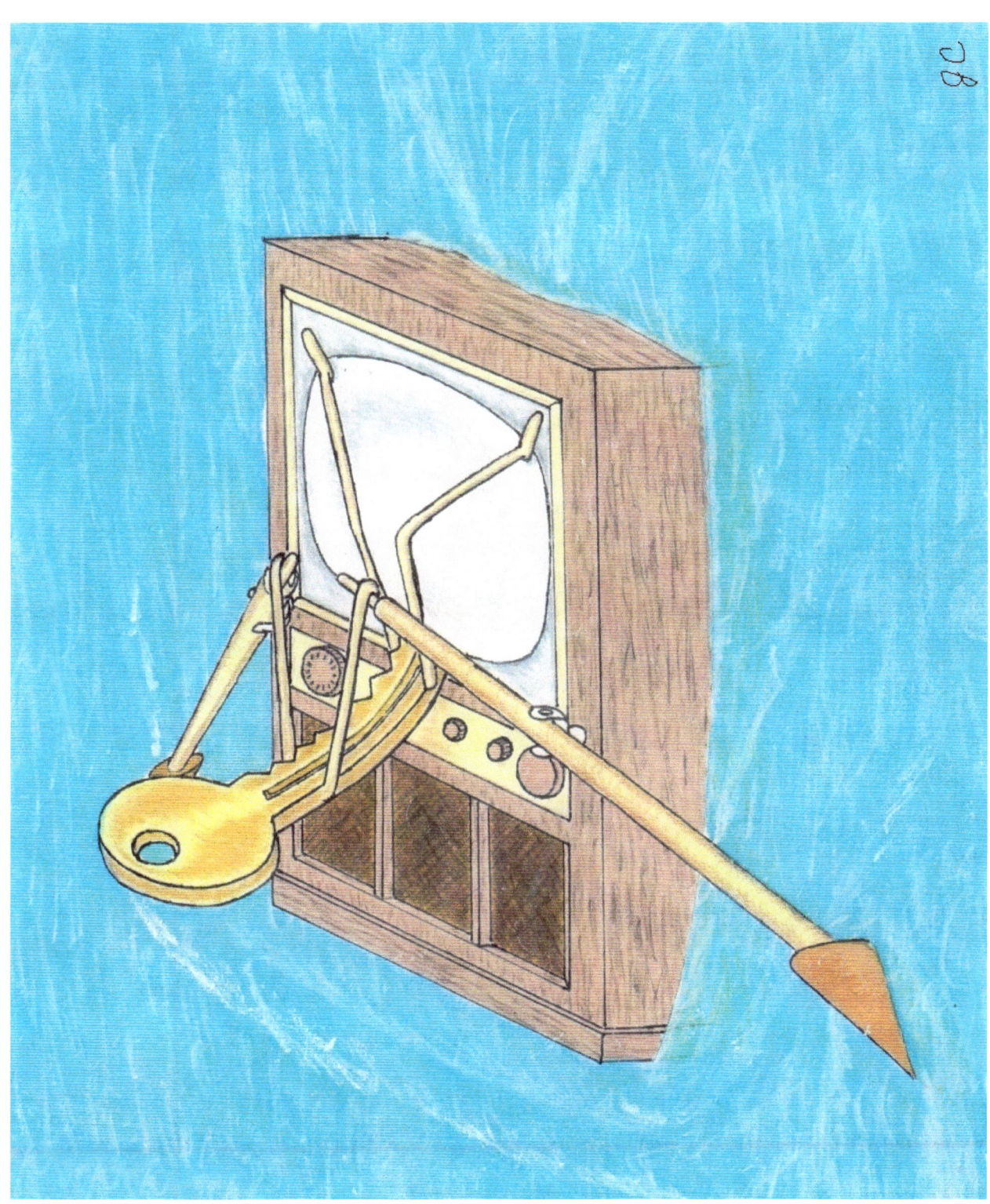

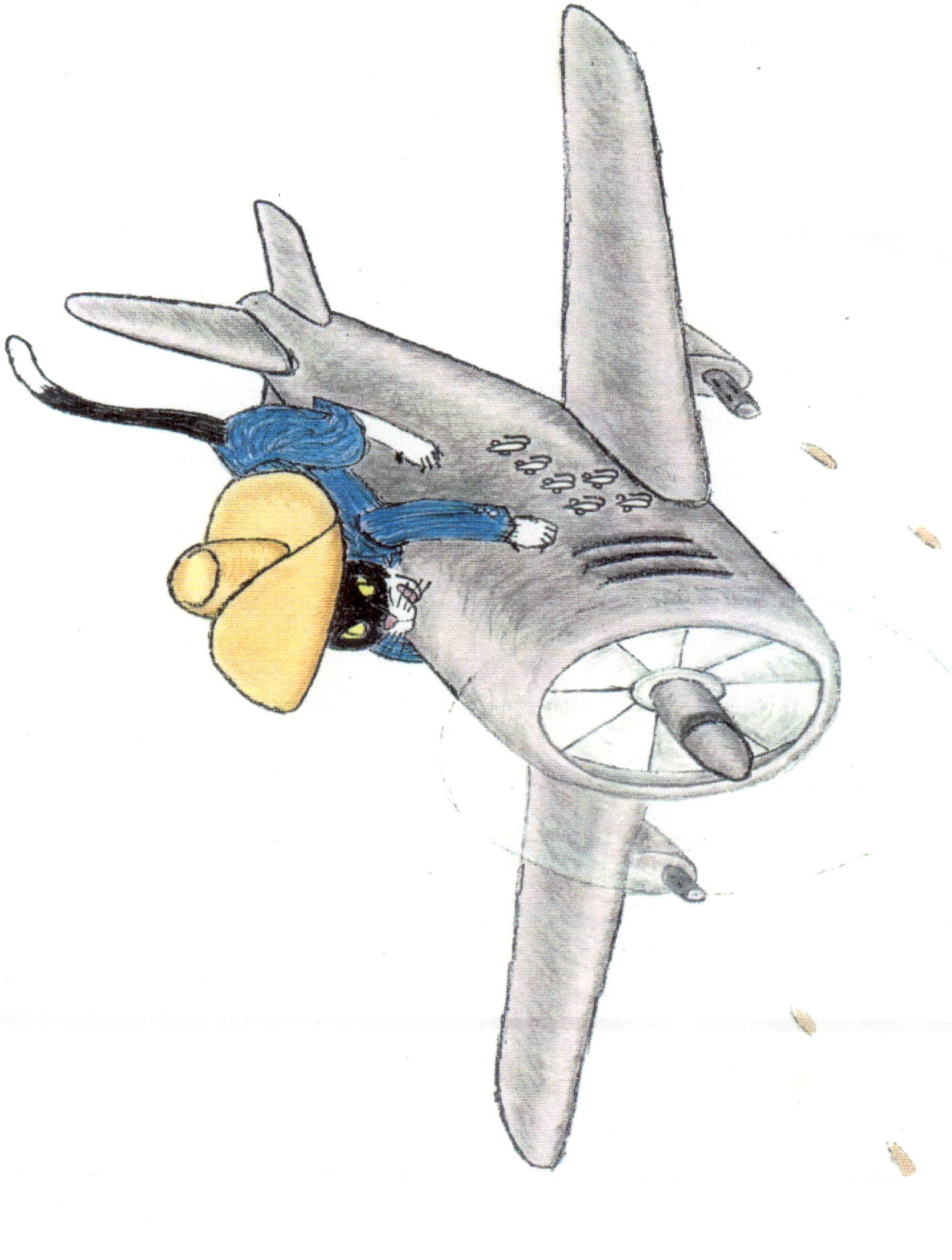

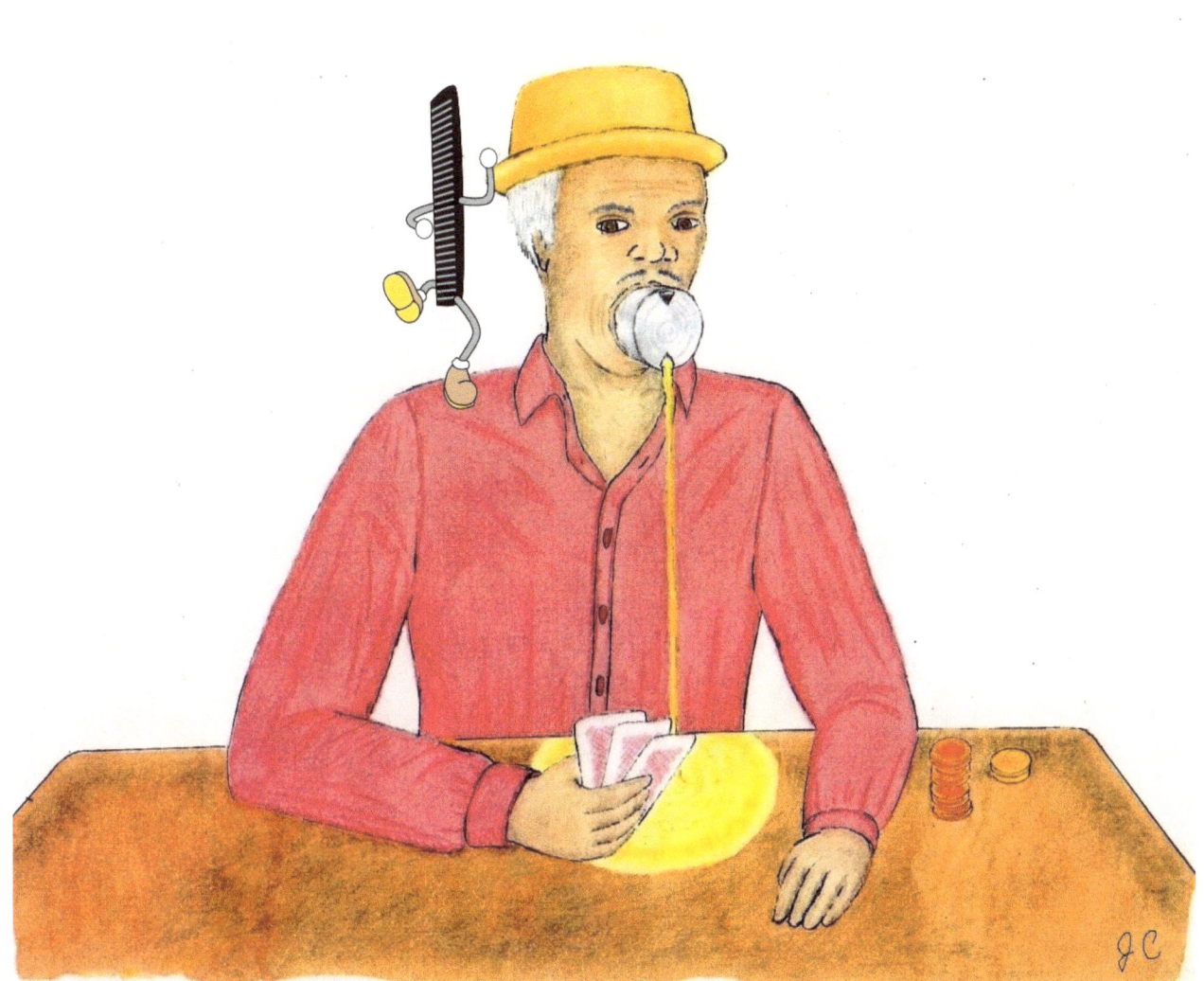

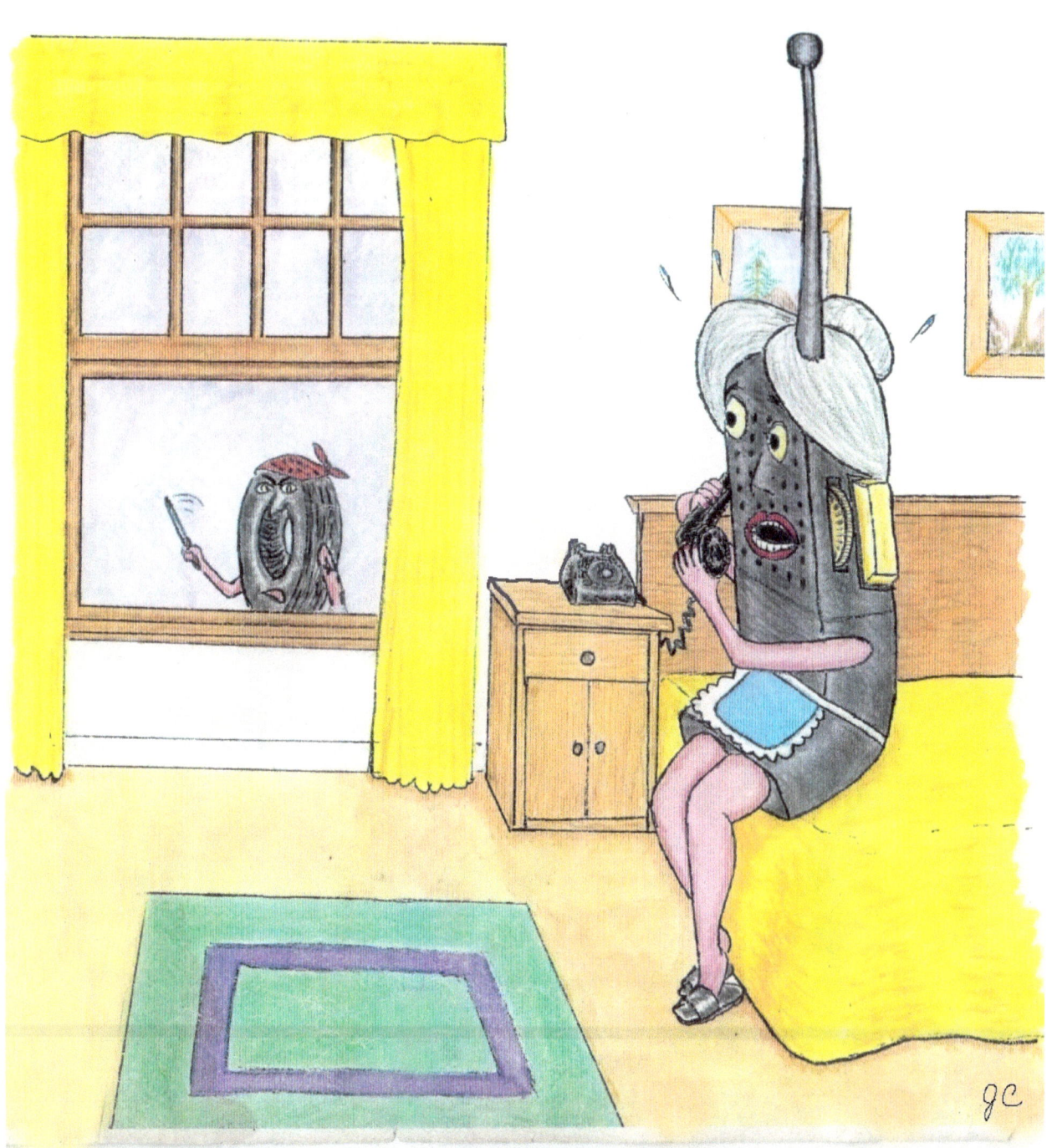

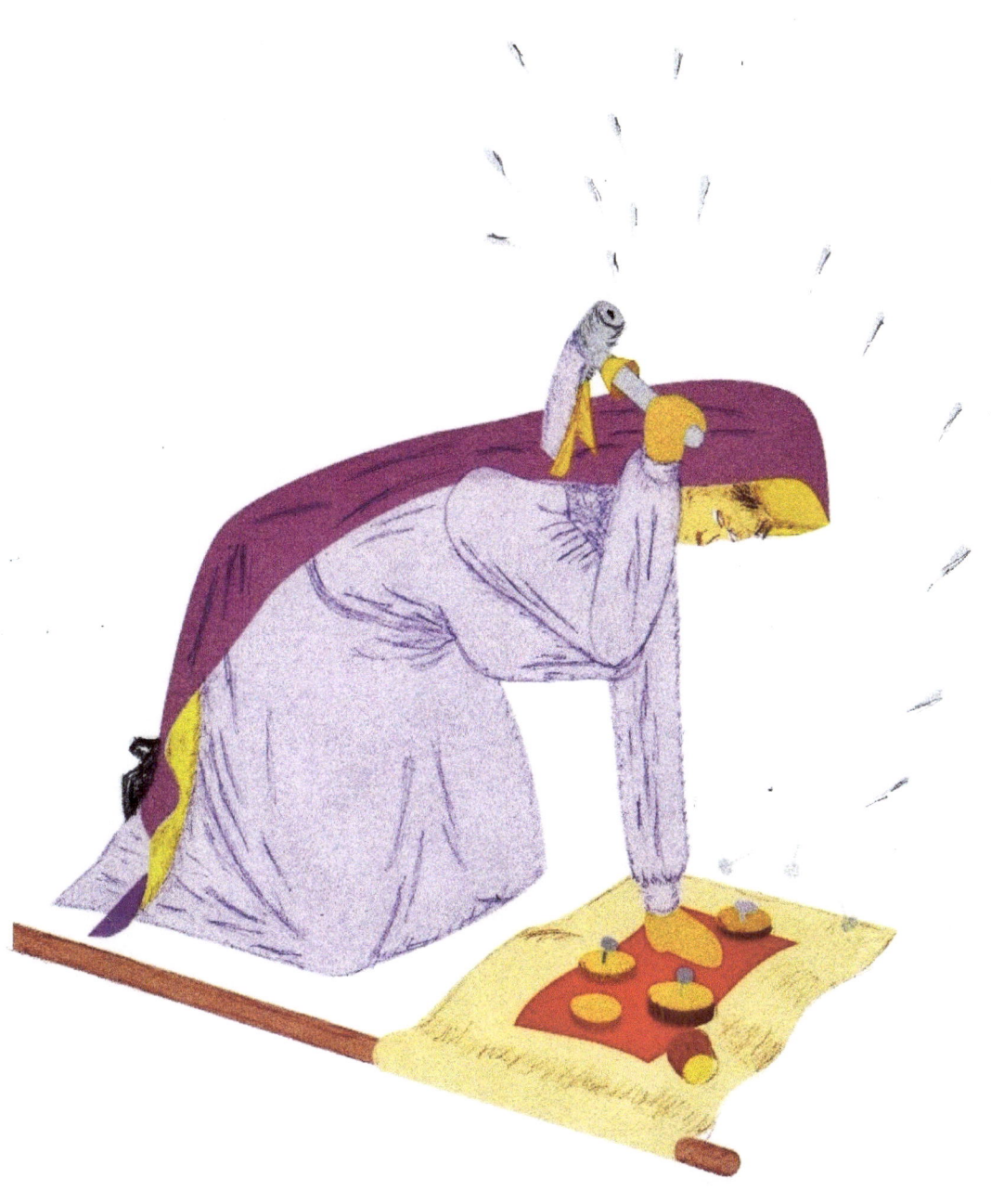

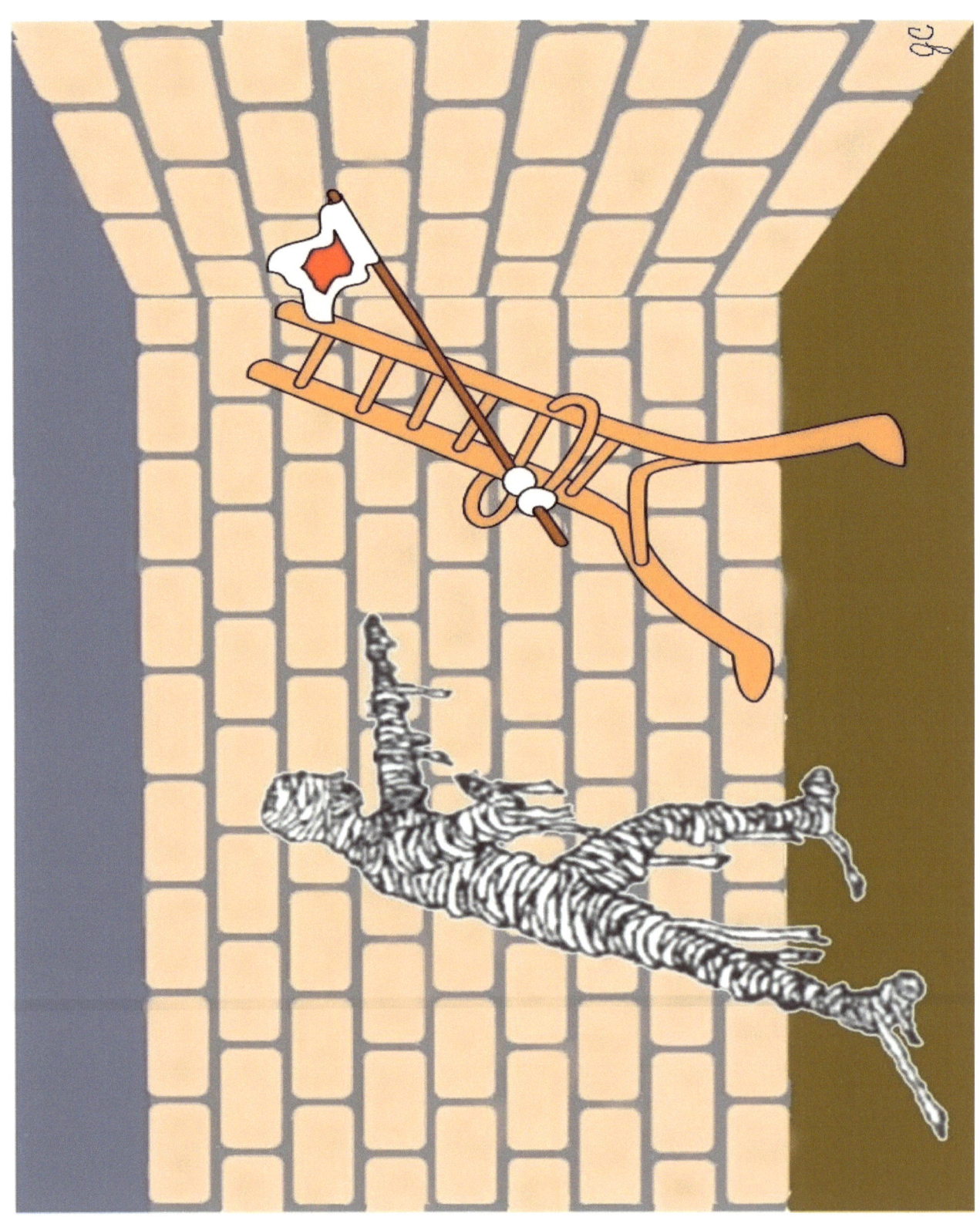

www.ingramcontent.com/pod-product-compliance
Lightning Source LLC
Chambersburg PA
CBHW050427180526
45159CB00005B/2434